I'M NOT FOR EVERYONE.

NEITHER ARE YOU.

David Leddick outside Grey Advertising, 1969

# I'M NOT FOR EVERYONE.

# NEITHER ARE YOU.

DAVID LEDDICK

Black Irish Entertainment LLC

NEW YORK                    LOS ANGELES

## Also by David Leddick

### FICTION

*My Worst Date*
*The Sex Squad*
*Never Eat In*
*The Handsomest Man in the World*
*The Millionaire of Love*
*I Don't Kiss*
*Love in the Loire*
*The Beauty of Men Never Dies*

### MALE NUDE PHOTOGRAPHY BOOKS

*Naked Men*
*Naked Men Too*
*The Male Nude*
*Male Nude Now*
*The Nude Male*
*Men in the Sun*
*Homoerotic Art of Pavel Tchelitchew*
*Gorgeous Gallery*

## MEMOIR

*We Offered Them Caviar*

## OTHER

*The Secret Lives of Married Men*
*Intimate Companions*
*Big Fun with Billy*
*George Platt-Lynes*
*Escort*
*How to Be Gay in the 21st Century*
*How to Hit 70 Doing 100*

BLACK IRISH ENTERTAINMENT LLC
ANSONIA STATION
POST OFFICE BOX 237203
NEW YORK, NY  10023-7203

FIRST BLACK IRISH ENTERTAINMENT TRADE
PAPERBACK EDITION MARCH 2014

FOR INFORMATION ABOUT SPECIAL DISCOUNTS
FOR BULK PURCHASES,
PLEASE VISIT WWW.BLACKIRISHBOOKS.COM

ISBN: 978-1-936891-19-1
EBOOK ISBN: 978-1-936891-23-8

PRINTED IN THE UNITED STATES OF AMERICA
1    2    3    4    5    6    7    8    9    10

For Vincent Colonna

"I thought I was looking for a man,
but it turned out I was looking for a manager."

# INTRODUCTION

## The Prince of 777 Third Avenue

My first job was in advertising in New York. David Leddick was my boss. Actually David wasn't my immediate supervisor; his station was so far above mine that he peeked through the clouds only occasionally, like Zeus or Oscar Wilde.

The year was 1966. David was thirty-five. I was twenty-three, newly married and fresh out of a six-month stint on active duty in the Marine Corps Reserve, with a buzz cut and a gray business suit that my Dad had bought me at Brooks Brothers, along with a pair of Johnston & Murphy wingtips. Such Mad Man fashion was not really necessary, as my job was as an assistant in the Traffic Department (i.e. office boy) at $105 a week.

The Revlon account was unique in the ad biz at that time. On a conventional piece of business like McDonald's or Chevrolet, the art directors and writers would be on one floor (the Creative Department), the account executives on another (Account Management) with the service provinces like Media and Research on their own floors.

On Revlon, we were all together. This was to concentrate the Jewish/fashionista/high-ambition hysteria and screw it to an unbearable pitch. I'm not kidding. By Friday evening, the deadline for ads going into next week's *Vogue* and *Elle* and *Cosmo*, the office's state of mind would be approaching collective psychosis.

Into this madness, David Leddick strode. He was Revlon's Worldwide Creative Director, and the only sane person within twenty blocks. "Now, children, let's see if we can dial back the dementia at least enough to preserve our livelihoods for the next seven days."

Amazingly, it worked. When David was in the house, all was well. He was the grown-up. The inmates had adult supervision.

David was the first—and at the time, the only—creative person in advertising to work under contract, not as a salaried employee. He demanded and got the perks of a superstar. David had been, among other things, manager of the Joffrey Ballet school, a TV director in Paris and a landowner on three continents. As an ad writer he was such a phenomenon that his portfolio displayed none of his actual work. Instead the tear sheets were all of *New Yorker* cartoons spoofing his ads. Again, I'm not kidding.

One of my jobs as an assistant traffic person was to deliver copy from the copywriters to the art directors. This involved walking into one office, picking up a piece of paper and carrying it into another office. All the copywriters on the Revlon account were women and they were all (so the secretaries declared) wildly overpaid. Each was a star in her own right.

Because cosmetic/fashion/hair color writing was so specialized, each gal writer was shrouded in mystery as to how she could do what she did. It took me three months to raise the nerve to actually glance at a sheet of ad copy as I hustled it down the hallway.

*The colors of autumn. Pungent. Pulse-pounding. Let your ragged heart take wing.*

I remember thinking:

1) "What is this?"

2) "I can write this shit."

David helped me put a portfolio together and made the phone call that got me a job as a junior writer. "I can't hire you here," he said. "If I did, you would always be remembered as the young man who used to carry copy from one office to another. Go elsewhere, make a name, then come back, if you dare."

I never did. My life broke into pieces sometime thereafter. I found myself on the road, down and out, blah blah etc.

Only David kept up with me. Twice a year I'd get a letter from him. He understood what had happened to me and, without ever alluding to it, made me feel that I was not as insane as I thought. He had been through this tunnel himself.

A few years later I was back in New York, driving a cab and tending bar. One afternoon on Park Avenue I spotted David, walking a few steps ahead of me. I was too ashamed to speak up. I ducked around the corner, cursing myself for being so gutless. Then a week later I was on the same street and saw David again. This time I had to speak.

It took David a few seconds to recognize me and another moment or two to assess my state of mind. "Why don't you let me take you to dinner?" That was the kind of gentleman David was, and is to this day.

David has been a mentor to dozens of young people, mostly artists and writers, dancers, actors, models. At critical points in their lives, he has proffered wisdom, made a phone call, even written a check. With me, it was one phrase. He told me something a dancer friend, a woman, had once said to him when they were both struggling:

> "David, we've been through some tough times but we always looked good and we were always fun to be with."

I don't know why that helped me so much. I certainly never looked good and was rarely fun to be with. Maybe that's why it helped. Because the world David inhabited— and his point of view within that world—was so different from mine.

David's world was about style and wit and not giving a damn what anybody thought of you. To be a gay man in 1966 was serious business; to be so, unapologetically and even flamboyantly, took real guts.

More than any person I've ever known, David is himself. His power comes from that center, which isn't trying to please you or be what you think it ought to be, or what anybody thinks it ought to be.

Much of David's work defies analysis. You can't break it down into its constituent elements. He did it. You can't. There it is.

In other words, David is an artist.

He has morals; he possesses a code. He helps people, he is unafraid. Whatever he does, he does with verve and élan and makes it seem like the hippest thing in the world, even though he couldn't care less what anybody thinks about him.

But perhaps the most amazing thing about David is his post-"retirement" productivity. Since 1995, David has written 25 books, including six novels and eight male nude photo studies. David is, in his own phrase, "the international guru of the male nude in photography." He has written art history, a major study of the photographer George Platt Lynes, and many more. In the year 2000, he returned to performing. He has appeared in six musicals, several of which he wrote himself. "My best review," he says, "was in *Some Men* by Terence McNally, when I sung *Somewhere Over the Rainbow* while wearing red feathers."

This is David, post-seventy years old.

All of David's books have been published by traditional entities. Sometimes they're small presses, occasionally university presses. But he always goes the Old School route. And David books his own tours. He sets dates at bookstores in New York, Chicago, San Francisco, Dallas, Atlanta, everywhere. Then promotes the events himself (he's got a very capacious Rolodex) and follows through, thanking everyone and keeping a database of all his contacts.

David is the absolute model of the artist/entrepreneur, who doesn't wait for anyone to give him permission to act. He does it all himself. How? I have no idea.

When Shawn Coyne and I started Black Irish Books, one of the first things I said was, "We gotta get David Leddick to write a book for us." I knew exactly what I wanted it to be. On the walls of David's office at Grey he had framed and hung a number of aphorisms, one- or two-line bits of wisdom that read, to me, like Zen koans. They were David's philosophy in bite size.

That's what this book is. That's how it's structured. Each chapter is short, sometimes only a paragraph. The chapter title is the axiom or maxim. For instance, one chapter is titled "Spend on the luxuries, the necessities will take care of themselves." Another is, "Before you leave the house, stop, look in the mirror—and take one thing off." A piece of wisdom from Coco Chanel. Then the rest of the chapter is David's explication upon that axiom. What does it mean? What's the logic underlying it? How do we apply it in our own lives?

The deeper question that I wanted David to answer—though I knew a) that it was unanswerable and b) that he would never consciously answer it)—was: How do you do it? What's the secret? What's your creative process? What is the essence of your style and your philosophy?

These, of course, are all the wrong questions to ask a person like David. If he were willing to answer them, he wouldn't be who he is.

If you've read my book, *The War of Art*, you know that my creative philosophy is blue-collar, no-nonsense, hard-core work ethic. David's style is the exact opposite. He produces work in prodigious quantities, but he does it in some, to me, magical way that never seems to raise a sweat. I'm baffled still.

Here is my first mentor, my first role model. Thank you, David. The first strands of my artistic DNA came from you. My hope is that the insights within these pages will serve the same function for those who read them.

Steven Pressfield
Los Angeles
2014

I'M NOT FOR EVERYONE.


NEITHER ARE YOU.

## Take One Thing Off

Coco Chanel said famously, "Before leaving the house, stop, look in the mirror—and take one thing off." This is a world philosophy in a nutshell. Pay attention please.

You are fine just the way you are. You need add no unnecessary extras. Don't think you have to present yourself to the world in added armor, disguised as someone else.

After all, how is someone going to fall in love with the real you unless the real you is present?

## In Defense of Style

Style is more than simple self-definition or a declarative statement of identity. Style is fun. Style is glamorous. Style is sexy. It is an exuberant embrace of life, through aesthetics.

Like the plumage of some great gorgeous bird, style says, "Here I am, come play with me."

## Fashion is not Style

The fields of fashion, beauty, and style are often dismissed as superficial, vain, narcissistic. Permit me to disagree.

Style is indivisible from authenticity, from being and becoming the "real you." It is the pursuit of authenticity that produces style. Style is the outer expression of an inner point of view, sense of humor, flair for expression.

Fashion comes and goes. Style is eternal.

What would you have worn at Versailles in the court of Louis the XIV? How would you have expressed yourself in Florence at the time of the Medicis? In a manner both stylish and distinctly your own, you may be sure, if you know who you are.

## Style and Identity

To ask "What is my style?" is to inquire "Who am I?"

## The Three Spheres of Style

What is your style? Do you have one? Remember, absence of style is a style too. It is a choice as well, which we make by default, defection, and abdication.

In my experience, there are three spheres through which we pass, and within which we act, on our passage through life. These are our inner life, our life with another, and our greater life among others.

Style is central to all three spheres.

It is the thesis of this book that in finding our style, we find ourselves. In expressing our style, we participate in and contribute to the world. In being our style, we discover and achieve our inherent individuality.

When we become who we were born to be, we express that essence through style.

So the next time you see a striking, fashionable woman or man gliding down the avenue, cut them some slack. The interior world they inhabit may not be as shallow or superficial as you imagine.

# Part One

Your Life On Your Own

**You need a style.**
**Your beauty cannot be your style.**

That eccentric philosopher and quipster Quentin Crisp always said in his monologues that beauty has a shelf life, while style can be forever. You have to find out who you are. And then the way you look, the way you talk, the way you present yourself says you, you, you.

People love singularity. And occasionally they hate it. But you will not be ignored by the world.

Perhaps you have a style. If not, think seriously about getting one. You don't want to be like everybody else.

**Style is not imposed, it is discovered.**

I don't believe in setting unchangeable goals because I don't believe we can see far enough ahead to know what we want. Life unfolds through action, which is why it is so important to follow your heart and to be brave. How can you set goals when you don't know what you'll find around the next corner? You meet someone and two months later you're living in another country, speaking a different language.

## When you lie awake,
## you are always seventeen.

Don't abuse yourself about your low-level of competence, intelligence, beauty or your fears of socializing, the future, money as you lay awake in the night. We all do it. Somehow we never get past being seventeen in the night.

But when you get up and go about your daily round, observe yourself. There you are solving this problem, dealing with that situation, all very capably. Even being fun when you feel like hell. You obviously aren't seventeen anymore.

You grew up.

Be proud of yourself for doing it.

**You can only feel for an hour and a half a day.**

Really. You can only muster your emotions and really focus on life for about an hour and a half a day. I used to go to ballet class every day for that fated hour and a half. I loved it. I concentrated on it. I was living fully and emotionally every minute I was there.

So the rest of the day? You are going to sleep for eight hours? Eat for three or four. That still leaves a good ten hours or more to fill. You might just as well get a job, pay the rent, earn a living.

Are you really feeling an hour and a half a day? Good for you, kiddo.

## "Leave your problems outside."

I studied ballet at the old Metropolitan Opera when Antony Tudor, the famous choreographer, was the head of the ballet school. In fact, Margaret Craske was the teacher most students considered to be more important. She had danced with Pavlova in the '20s.

Miss Craske instructed us: "Leave your problems outside the classroom."

Such good advice. And in that hour and a half of intense concentration on every part of your body, the music, the coordinating with other dancers you really couldn't think about your troubles and it was great escaping them. You emerged much more relaxed and self-confident.

We worked hard. We never had a sick day. You went on even if you had to lie down in the wings until you were needed. No one thought this was unusual.

At the Met, the powers that be were only interested in two things: how well you sang and how well you danced. Your race didn't count, your background, sexual preferences, family, none of that mattered. You had to deliver. That was the sole standard. It was great.

In later careers all of this has stood me in good stead. I never had to work that hard in any of the various worlds I entered. I knew the quality of the work I was doing. Dancing at the Met was a wonderful experience and a wonderful preparation for the rest of my life.

## Sell it somewhere else

Miss Craske taught the Cecchetti Method, a ballet technique created by Enrico Cecchetti, who had trained the Russian greats: Nijinsky, Pavlova, Karsavina and many others.

She was an English lady with a high, piercing voice. She brooked no foolishness in her classes. One day my friend Betty Ann Paulin, who was a musical comedy dancer, was in the front row doing a combination of dance steps.

Miss Craske stopped the class and said, "Betty Ann, you wretched girl, what are you doing?" Betty Ann replied, "I'm selling it, Miss Craske."

Then came the reply: "Well, you can sell it somewhere else."

At the Met, you were there to serve the music, the story, and the production. Never your own ego.

## "Star" and "nice" have nothing to do with each other.

I appeared onstage for the first time in the debut of the legendary soprano Maria Callas. I probably appeared in every opera she sang at the Met except *Madame Butterfly*. (No dancers in that one.)

Miss Callas never spoke to anyone else in the cast. She sang at her co-stars, not with them. She never spoke to them either. Marlene Dietrich was waiting for her at lunchtime. She was that kind of star.

Callas was a great, moving, transcendent performer who sang unforgettably. I think she was scarcely aware that other people existed.

You must not expect that from those who provide beauty and glamour and intellect to our world either.

# TROUSER ROLES

When Miss Craske worked with Pavlova in the '20s, she often danced the trouser roles. Trouser roles were those in which girls danced men's parts. Since the days of Nijinksy, there has been a dearth of men in the world of ballet.

I've often wondered why. Leaving class, one would see macho types loitering on street corners and "regular guys" on their way to drinks or the office. Clearly they would sooner step into traffic than attend the ballet, or God forbid, take part.

Classes at the Met were conducted in the old opera house on the fifth floor in a large two-story space. Up front were huge framed mirrors. The pianist sat off to the left. Ballet barres were fastened to the three other walls. The dressing rooms were in the back up a short flight of stairs. All was exactly as it had been in the days of Pavlova and Nijinsky.

The ballet company rehearsed in this studio and another equally large one on the other side of the stage. These two spaces were linked by a narrow walkway that hung in space over the gigantic Metropolitan stage, some five stories below. It was vertiginous to pass from one studio to the other.

When I was there I lived in a four-room cold-water flat in Chelsea, for which I paid $25.00 a month. Heat was a gas stove in the kitchen. When you turned on the oven and left the door open it would heat the kitchen and a small adjoining room. The apartment was a "railroad flat" with the rooms running in a row, front to back, four in all. There were four apartments to each floor, sharing a toilet in the hall on each floor. In the kitchen was a large bathtub with metal covers that came down, which served as a work table when no one was using it to take a bath.

My furniture was largely found on the street, specifically a kitchen table with folding wings and two chairs that I kept for years afterwards. I remember passing the table in the street and thinking "I'm not that desperate." Then getting home and saying to myself as I looked about, "Yes, I am."

My day was to be in the Opera house by ten in the morning. I had a direct ride from the 14th street station of the Seventh Avenue subway right up to 42nd street. There was an exit at 40th street by the stage door. There was a fruit stand there. We all usually bought an apple or an orange as we entered. I had a gray sweater and gray corduroy pants that I wore every day as I only had them on for the subway ride there and back much later that night.

The opera of course was a repertory house, so every day there were rehearsals for upcoming productions. We reported in at ten, rehearsed to four with a lunch break, then went to class from four-fifteen until five-forty-five. The more ambitious then went to a second class at six and dashed to the dressing room at seven-thirty for an eight o'clock curtain. We almost always were there for the entire production, which would finish between eleven and midnight.

We particularly disliked Wagner's *Die Meistersinger* as it ran until after midnight. I can remember looking out over the audience, which was almost entirely empty by the time the curtain came down.

We worked with big stars like Maria Callas, Eleanor Steber, Lisa Della Casa, Patrice Munsel. They were all there. Miss Callas paid no attention to anyone but was by far the greatest star. Eleanor Steber won our undying affection in a rehearsal for *Don Giovanni* when, wearing a low-cut street dress she flung herself down on the body of her father and her ample bosom popped out into the eyes of the startled orchestra, which came to a fumbling stop. She laughed, rearranged herself and said, "Let's do this scene again."

And we all loved the beautiful Lisa Della Casa. I remember standing behind her ready to go on at the very end of a seemingly endless opera. It was late and we were all dead tired. She looked back over her shoulder and said, "Let's go, kids." And go we went.

We went to the shower rooms and were painted all over when we performed in *Aida*. We wore practically nothing except huge headdresses and it was always freezing onstage as the sets were so huge they had to open the gigantic street doors on the back of the theater to bring them in. The doors had to be left open as the sets had to be left out on Seventh Avenue if not in use. Whatever the temperature was outdoors, it was the same on stage.

The stage manager called the nearly naked male dancers "The Sex Squad." We used to huddle in a corridor offstage to avoid the winter chill onstage. The manager would put his head in the door and call "Sex Squad!" when it was time to go on. Brrrrrr. Then we would rush back to the corridor once we left the stage.

We did all this work, work, work six days a week with a matinee on Saturday. Two performances that day. On Sundays I usually rehearsed with another company, performing modern dance.

Being a man in ballet, filling the trouser roles, was certainly disdained by the typical male of the 50s or 60s. But I will challenge any linebacker or test pilot to do what we did, to do it in all weathers, under all emotional conditions, and to do it with such unflagging good humor.

**There is little difference between success and failure.**

I have probably failed at everything I really wanted to do in life. And have had a certain level of success at the second-best level. I think success and failure feel pretty much the same. What is important is that you tried. An awful lot of people suffer from "fear of failure" which keeps them from trying to do stuff. I assure you when you have failed, if you fail, you are not going to go around kicking yourself. You will feel pretty good that you tried. You will say "There, that's out of the way. What's next?"

When you realize that success and failure are virtually the same thing, it's very liberating. Get out there and fail!

## "Never complain. Never explain."

Elsie de Wolfe? Bet you never heard of her. A young woman of good family and no money who became an actress, sometime before 1900. Elsie lived with the Broadway producer Bessie Marbury. Lesbians? Maybe.

Elsie took a Red Cross unit of nurses to France in World War I, was given a medal by the French government and married Lord Mendl, an official at the English Embassy in Paris. She became a Lady. Their sex life? Her husband is reported to have said, "The old girl could be a virgin for all I know."

Elsie escaped Paris one step ahead of the Nazis with Lord M., her secretary, her car and her jewels by way of Spain and Portugal and took ship to the United States. She promptly went to Los Angeles and continued her decorating career with great success. At ninety, she stood on her head every day. I learned that from her. She said, "The important thing is to remain supple." Indeed.

Elsie returned to Paris after the war and kept right on entertaining and decorating. She had her face lifted a number of times, much to her chauffeur's approval.

Her credo was, "Never complain, never explain." I have followed in her footsteps.

No one wants to know.

No one needs to know.

**Fashion is when you dress for others.
Style is when you dress for yourself.**

Acquaintances in New York were often surprised to learn
that I, whose professional and personal world revolved
around fashion and glamour, was a passionate devotee of
Zen meditation. I told them, "They are the same thing."

I would go upstate on week-long *sesshins*, where you
sat all day in meditation, ate in silence, and padded off
to your humble chamber without a glance or a word to
anyone. Then rose at four-thirty the next morning to
begin again.

No one possesses greater style than a Zen monk. He
or she simply is. I marveled at the power of beauty and
glamour that can be generated by simply sitting still and
being oneself.

P.S. One might replace "dress" with "act" in the
subject line above, as well.

## "Don't be selfish, think of your career."

An admonition to Mae West from her mother when she didn't want to take a movie role she thought was beneath her.

If you don't want to do something because you imagine it offends you, offends others, offends everyone, think twice. Maybe you're just being selfish trying to spare yourself some of the difficulties of life. Come on. The more bad stuff you deal with, the more your karma owes you good stuff.

**Don't ask for a raise.**
**Get a better job and come back as a star.**

Or perhaps don't come back at all. You will always make more money moving to another job than expecting to be rewarded by your present employer. Don't be hesitant about the new. Go for it. Clamber upward as fast as you can.

I loved what Sharon Stone said when asked impertinently by an interviewer if she had slept her way to the top. She replied, "I slept my way to the middle. I clawed my way to the top." Sharon, you go. And *you* go, too.

**Spend on the luxuries.**
**The necessities will take care of themselves.**

When I was working in New York in an early job I bought a beautiful French desk for $600. That was a lot of money in the 1960s. All the money I had in the world. I told myself I could ride the subway and skip taking taxis. Having that desk made me feel that I was creating the life around me that I wanted.

Pinching your pennies may make sense to you, but you are missing that feeling of being a grand person living a grand life. Go ahead and take that trip to Paris. You'll never regret it. Somehow you will take care of the necessities. Don't worry about it.

Is there a life you imagine for yourself in the future? Start living it now. Project yourself materially into that future self, that expectant world. You'll be surprised how the real world will catch up.

**Let us not complain.
It makes us so unattractive.**

Fake it and pretend you have no problems. It will make other people very jealous of you.

Somehow the act of pretending lowers the level of problems you actually have.

**When you lead a secret life,
the only one it's secret to is you.**

Your alcoholism, your sexual preference. You think no one knows.

Everyone knows.

They're just being polite.

## After a while your problems become your lifestyle.

As Miss Craske admonished us to leave our problems outside the classroom, I might add leave your problems outside entirely.

First you bring up your troubles with your mother or once in a while with your friends. Then you're calling them late at night. Your problems have become you, and you have become your problems.

One friend used to call me late and yammer on and on while I read, putting the phone on my shoulder. When I heard a pause I'd pick up and say, "Is that so?" or "Really?" Finally after some years of this I said,"You know, Phyllis, no one really wants to hear your problems."

She replied, "Do you think I don't know that and I don't care?"

Exactly.

**Most problems go away when you throw money at them.**

Talking tough, money does solve a great many problems when they are brought to you by others. Instead of having to hear endless complaints from a friend about not being able to pay the rent, you just pay it for them. Then you don't have to avoid them. The complaints are over, at least for the time being.

More seriously, nothing is worse than having someone you love and care about need medical attention and they can't afford it. Step up to bat and pay for that operation, medication, whatever. You'll always like yourself for having done it. You will dislike yourself to the end of your days for not having done it.

Trite but true: If you can pay for the solution, you haven't got a problem.

## THE ADVERTISING AGE

I was in and out of advertising for forty years. When I first came to New York in 1955 I worked at Kenyon & Eckhardt on RCA Victor Television. I left to dance and returned in 1958 to work for Batten, Barton, Durstine and Osborne, then J. Walter Thompson into the 60s.

I managed the Robert Joffrey Ballet School for a year or so before coming back to work for Hockaday Associates, then Norman, Craig and Kummel, Smith and Dorian and on to Grey Advertising.

Having many jobs does not speak poorly of you in advertising. If you're a talented creative person, competing agencies are always looking for you. If they have a client who is a competitor of your client they particularly want you for what you know.

If you stay too long at one agency it is often thought to be suspicious. You aren't talented enough to be sought out for other jobs.

Remember, you can always make a lot more money moving to a new agency than trying to get a raise where you are now. People pop around a lot on their upward climb.

I settled at Grey as I was the Worldwide Creative Director for Revlon, one of the agency's premium accounts. Revlon spent 40 some million a year on advertising at that time. A gigantic fortune by today's standards. Of that the agency got 17%. That was a lot of moolah. *Advertising Age*, the trade magazine, used to publish a list of the ten worst clients every year. Revlon was always number one.

I was lucky. When I danced we worked from ten in the morning to midnight six days a week. Revlon was easier than that. I went to work at 10:30 knowing I would be working late. I went to the gym on my lunch hour to get it out of the way. We met with the client every day. The workload was enormous. Always half a dozen television commercials and ten or more magazine ads were in the works. We did all the advertising for the whole world as Revlon wanted it all to be the same everywhere. It was a lot of work.

Revlon was a lot more like Hollywood than Madison Avenue. The current TV show *Mad Men* doesn't really capture the pace and pressure of clients like Revlon.

The president was the fabled Charles Revson, a famous cranky person. He was a genius and a self-made man, starting out making nail enamel in a bathtub. Meetings at Revlon usually involved a lot of cursing and remarks like, "You used to have talent but now you're all washed up." Somehow it never bothered me. I kept signs on my wall to encourage my staff. One read "The Trick is Not Caring."

What that meant was being emotionally bulletproof.

You had to know what you had done was good and if the client didn't like it you just tucked it away and brought it back another time. I always told people who worked for me that their self-esteem had to be kept in their own hands. They were never going to get any compliments or approval from this client. Revlon was never going to like anything. But the fact they kept those forty plus millions with us was the testimony that we were doing fine.

I reminded my writers and art directors that Coco Chanel said,"I never designed a good dress until I didn't care anymore."

You don't have to care to be a top grade professional. What you do have to do is never let yourself down and always do top grade work. I had another framed quotation on the wall that read,"We are all in the gutter but some of us are looking at the stars." Oscar Wilde. Just because you are dealing with difficult people does not mean that you must become like them. You manipulate them, you deal with them, you finally learn to get what you want as an end goal. If there was one thing that I wanted my staff to learn from me it was,"I am willing to lose battles as long as I win the war."

Revlon themselves understood this. They were very difficult. They were very demanding. But if you could do the work you got the job. Women held important positions at Revlon. Kay Daly, Revlon's in-house Creative Director, was the most highly paid woman in the United States. She earned $100,000 a year back in the 1960s. I can only guess what that would be today.

Working for Revlon, you could be black, you could be gay, you could be anything but if you could do the job you got it. They didn't care what school you went to, what family you came from, how wealthy your background. That meant nothing if you couldn't do the work. Grey Advertising was essentially the same kind of company. I always felt they were truly American. I had a French friend visit from Paris once and he said,"The great thing about this country is that you feel anything is possible."

I was Worldwide Creative Director for Revlon for twenty years. They were always willing to spend a lot of money to accomplish something excellent. They complained every step of the way but we all knew where we were going.

In the early 1970s I had spent a couple of years in Paris working as a director of television commercials. I loved France, I loved Paris. My dream had always been to speak French and live in Paris. By the time I was forty I had accomplished this. My only true life goal. The rest has all been dessert.

I went back to Paris in 1985 to be International Creative Director for L'Oreal. I always worked under contract and was there for three years working at McCann-Erickson Advertising. In this case the client liked me fine but the agency hated having a foreigner who actually spoke French in any kind of management position. The French are a curious race. At first they didn't like me because I didn't speak French. Then they didn't like me because I spoke French with an accent. Finally they said,

"It isn't nice when a foreigner speaks French without an accent." If they weren't going to like you they weren't going to like you and that was that.

I used my Revlon technique on them. "The Trick is Not Caring." I really didn't care what they thought and it worked fine.

Finally after four years I was done at McCann-Erickson and worked between the United States and Europe as a free-lance creative director. At 65 I wrote my first novel, and *eh, voila,* there I was off on yet another career.

Looking for the perfect word.

**I will do anything for money.
The less I like to do it, the more it costs.**

This goes back to my days with Revlon in advertising. I would find myself in meetings with the cosmetic giant's staff and say to myself, "What am I doing here with all these crazy people?" Then I would say, "You are being paid a lot of money to be here, that's why you are here."

It made me relentless with my employer, Grey Advertising. Every year my price went up. And rightly so. If you are capable of doing work that others are not, be sure you are paid well for it. It really makes it possible to bear up.

## Elegance is the ability to say no.

This quotation comes from Coco Chanel. Elegance, she believed, is not only how you look. It is how you behave.

Elegance is the ability to present yourself to the world stripped down to the real you. Without subterfuge. When you say no, you are refusing to be anything other than who you are, or to look or seem any way other than your authentic being. You say no to pretending you are someone other than who you are.

**Think it but don't say it.**

I often carry on imagined conversations in my head. What I will say to someone next time we meet. That I am unhappy about their behavior. Reminding them of something they said that was uncalled for. In general pulling up the discords and talking it out with them.

I have learned to have these conversations in my head and leave them there.

They will only evoke conventional responses; only continue your manner of relating to that other person. Better to say nothing. In that way you have some chance of interrupting the give and take that is formulaic in your relation with them and perhaps heading off in a whole new direction.

Think it. Don't say it.

## "Don't tell us what you think, tell us what you feel."

Revlon used to say this to me when they were an advertising client. A bunch of toughies in the beauty business but they knew what they were doing. I would come back from a tour of Europe and say, "I think…" and they would respond with the above. Then I would say, "For next Autumn I see 'Plum'." That's what they wanted to hear. They knew that the subconscious was collecting information as I traveled around talking to beauty makers and seeing fashion around the continent. They knew there was an impression more important than what I might rationally conclude.

It's true. When you flash on something, it is your subconscious sending you the message it has been mulling over. Listen to it.

## "I never designed a good dress until I didn't care anymore."

Talent and emotional involvement are two different things. When Coco Chanel uttered the quotation above, she spoke a profound truth. When you truly become professional, you know when your work is good. You don't need others to tell you.

When I worked in advertising I used to return from client meetings and say, "We offered them caviar but they wanted peanut butter." We didn't need the client to tell us something was good. We knew. We had to be above rejection and approval. We *knew* it was good. We didn't have to care.

Consider Marilyn Monroe. All she needed was one good friend to say, "You are a great comic actress. Go do your thing. Don't try to be Sarah Bernhardt. She's dead. Be yourself at your best."

Unfortunately Marilyn didn't have that friend to tell her.

You should tell yourself that. You know yourself at your best. You don't need someone else's approval. And you can ignore any rejection you get from others. They don't know as well as you do. I promise.

**Don't wish revenge upon someone. Wish them a long life.**

The Spanish have a saying, "Revenge is a dish best served cold." How about *very* cold?

Don't be hovering about wishing someone the worst. It just makes you less of a person. Just hope they have a long life. I promise you they won't enjoy it.

**Don't get off the train at the wrong station.
It's very hard to get back on.**

I do see life as a journey. I think frequently out of fear or a need for security people get off at the wrong station. They marry someone because all their friends are getting married. They stay in a job where they are not particularly happy, even when offered a different and perhaps better one. They stop moving forward. When they want to move forward later, it is often too late.

They are too embedded in that station where they got off the train of life. They cannot get up and get on the train again.

## "I have lived my life for glamour and beauty and it has brought me here."

When I was a Zen student at Dai Bosatsu Zendo in New York City we were required to speak from time to time on Thursday nights, when the first timers came to visit. The above was how I always started my speech.

The meditation room itself, stripped bare except for black floor cushions and a candle burning at the front of the room, was stripped down elegance. There was also the fact that there was no dogma. Everything you learned had to come from yourself. From deep within your own psyche, your own subconscious.

To me Zen meditation was the final exploration of why beauty causes the excitement of glamour and why it happens within us. Stimulated by other people perhaps, but we ourselves are the ones having the feelings.

Once you start the fuse of meditation burning it continues to sizzle for the rest of your life.

**Don't let the life you want
keep you from getting the life you need.**

I have meditated for quite a few years, many of them at Dai Bosatsu Zendo in New York City. Zen is not a religion but a spiritual discipline. There is no dogma. What you learn you teach yourself. There were times in the hours of meditation, which could be very physically painful— your knees, your back—when a small bell would ring and you could go talk briefly to the Roshi. When asked about the pain he once responded to me,"It goes away, doesn't it?"

The only thing the Roshi ever said to me for guidance was, "Don't be so sure that what you want is what you should have."

This gave me a sense of my destiny. It reassured me that what is delivered to me or taken from me is the road I am somehow predestined to take. The obstacle must be overcome to get to the fulfillment and goodness waiting for you.

In some way someone or some force is watching over you. And I now also believe, the further down you go the further up you will travel in the future. Lots of bad luck is like money in the bank. Lots of good luck awaits you.

## ZEN STUDIES

I started my Zen studies when I was 40. A friend, Rinaldo Frattilillo, who was studying Comparative Religion at the New School in New York, called me. "We're going to visit a Zen center tomorrow night. You're always talking about Zen. Come along." I did. Rinaldo never returned. I did. I loved the large empty room with just a candle burning at one end, the two rows of people meditating. I particularly loved it when a slightly cantankerous student said to the Roshi or Abbot during the talk period, "Why do the men and women sit on opposite sides of the room?" and he replied, "Because there is no difference." I also love quick-witted people.

I attended Thursday nights for the required period and then was allowed to come, sit down on a black cushion, fold my legs and just sit for two 40-minute periods, walking a bit in between. No speaking, no sermons, no nothing, just me, and complete silence. You never really meet anyone in Zen studies. Students don't speak to each other. There is never any need or opportunity.

In about six months I attended a weekend meditation. It started on a Friday evening at seven o'clock and continued until Sunday evening. Meditation until ten o'clock, a sleeping bag until 4:30 a.m. for two nights. Five to seven is early meditation, eating and cleaning without speaking or looking at anyone. No one mentions that meditation is so – painful. No one warns you of this. Those people who meditate sitting on an easy chair? Forget it. That's not meditation. Dozing maybe. Meditation is hard work but the pain keeps you from having drifting thoughts. You fight your way through each 40-minute period, praying to hear that little bell that lets you stand up.

In about a year I tackled a weeklong meditation at the monastery in the Catskill Mountains. Several years later I talked with a Zen student who came from Japan. He did the week meditation and then told me, "This continues the Japanese tradition. There is nothing this difficult still being done in Japan." It was from five in the morning until ten at night for seven days. Forty minute intervals broken by meals at long tables where you do not speak or look at anyone.

Cleaning in the monastery basement one morning I ran across the cat some student had brought along. I could look at him and speak to him. "Here kitty," I said and started to cry. After the first day you forget about your laundry and the people you had forgotten to call. At the end of the second day you have gone through all the thoughts about your mother, lovers, etc. At the end of the third day you only think about escaping through the snow and hitchhiking back to New York. About the fourth day you are really emptied out because of no interaction with other people. You sit down, your knees hurt, and you think of nothing, the bell rings. One could talk to the Roshi. I told him, "The pain in my knees is terrible." He said, "Does it go away when you stand up?" I admitted it did. He said, "Well?"

**David Leddick and Zen Guru at the Mountain Monastery**

After about four years of meditating each morning for twenty minutes before going to work, attending Dai Bosatsu Zendo in New York at least one night a week, plus weekends in the city, and full weeks in the mountains, I finally had an insight. I realized that I was very peripheral to whatever was going on here in this life. I told this to the Roshi and he said I was heading in the right direction. I said, "I don't know that I want to be one with the universe." He replied, "You don't have a thing to worry about."

I still meditate each morning, finding that it returns me to a kind of good-tempered view towards where I find myself. What other people experience with meditation I can never know. And I am highly suspect of those who talk about it. Perhaps I have even said too much here.

**I thought I was learning how to live,
then I realized I was learning how to die.**

This did not originate from me but very nicely synopsizes my thinking about living your life to the fullest. I think when you really try to explore yourself and your potential you see it as a learning process. When it comes time to check out you realize that you can die with no regrets if you have tried to find out who you are and have acted upon what you have learned.

There is nothing more to do. It is time to go.

## What I admire most is courage.

It's the greatest of all qualities. Courage. We are all afraid but we should never let ourselves down and shy away from the things we fear. Courage lets us progress. Even more important, it lets us be proud of ourselves. Makes us stronger in our ability to face each new challenge. Courage, my friends. Take courage.

## "There is no lasting comfort in a safe landing. Better to stay in flight ... and embrace impermanence."

I was surprised to find this quote from Mr. Frank Langella, whose memoir *Dropping Names* tells you a lot about the famous people he knew but not a lot about himself. He can hardly have been just an observing nonentity passing through these other people's lives and somehow his conclusion after all that was to "embrace impermanence." It's what I call staying on the train of life. He says it very well.

Frank Langella has a wonderful story about Bette Davis. He had spoken to her a number of times on the phone. He found her seated in a hotel lobby and told her how much he admired her and her work. She said "Thank you." Then to remind her that they had spoken he leaned down and said, "It's Frank Langella." Without looking at him she puffed on her cigarette and replied, "I said 'Thank you.' Great. Talk about dismissive.

# Part Two
Your Life With A Lover

## "You Need a Look"

When Maria Callas taught at Juilliard she frequently told her students this. A great voice is not enough. I can testify to this. I was dancing at the Metropolitan Opera at exactly the seasons that Maria Callas sang there.

Callas had been a heavy-set girl from Brooklyn, who got trapped in Greece during World War II. She emerged, married the aged millionaire Menenghini, lost a ton of weight and arrived on the scene like a dramatic bombshell.

She was absolutely astonishing onstage. She created the atmosphere in which the entire production took place. Everything the audience felt you also felt if you were onstage with her. She had a look like some kind of fantastic snake goddess.

That was a star.

She had a look.

You need a look.

## Navy blue is always better than brown.

This is your eternal fashion tip. You will always look better in navy blue than brown. With white around the face. Don't ask me why. I have observed this thousands of times. This does not translate to lighter tones in warmer weather.

Beige is better than light blue. Again, don't ask me why.

This is just the observation from the former Worldwide Creative Director for Revlon. As I always tell my friends,"But what would I know about fashion?"

## Never chase someone who should be chasing you.

My Uncle Sidney said, "Never chase a streetcar or a woman. There'll be another one along in a minute." Well, the streetcars are gone but the idea is there. If someone isn't interested in you they are not going to become more so by your persistence.

You dropping the chase, abruptly, might in fact result in piquing their interest in you. Come on. You're top notch. People should be chasing you.

**Love is never impossible.**


And I am not talking about your love for your child, your nephew, your cat or your dog.

I am talking about romantic love. The love that makes you feel you have been recognized as a one-of-a-kind special human being by another human being. Who wants to team up with you against the world. The team where one and one makes so much more than two. The team that makes you feel, "There. I have lived. I have been fulfilled."

If it hasn't happened yet do not give up. Keep your eyes open. Think about whom it is that you can fall in love with. If your choice is truly impossible (a movie star, some person you do not even know, a storybook character, etc.) sit down and think about it. When your choice is the impossible dream then you are at fault. Keep your eyes open. Someone out there is looking for you.

## A bad review is just one person's opinion.

I'm a writer and a bad review does not bother me. Honestly. I know it is just one person and they have every right in the world to not like my book. They may influence other people but Kismet, it is written in the stars.

I think this is true of all criticism. Don't let it bother you. It's just one person. I am sure there are hundreds who think you are swell.

**"David, we've been through some tough times but we always looked good and we were always fun to be with."**

My great friend Norma Stevens said this to me years ago. Norma and I trained as dancers at the same time at the Met, toiled in summer stock at the same theater, and later worked in advertising at the same time. Long-term New Yorkers through a number of loves and the ups-and-downs of growing up, we both learned that no one is interested in your problems. Also, that most people are attracted to you by the way you look and by your consistent good temper.

Friends may be willing to hear your problems and sympathize. They may even be supportive. But they become bored quickly. Face it, the only one who can deal with your problems is you.

You are better off seeming to be problem-free and full of fun. I promise you, no one needs to know otherwise.

**In confrontation, never answer the way people expect you to.**

When you are having a disagreement with someone, it is something like a tennis match. The ball goes back and forth over the net. You say one thing. The other person responds exactly as they are expected to. Nothing advances. No one is convinced. No minds are changed. Round and round it goes in a pattern of repetition.

Don't do this. Just think what they expect you to say in response and don't do it. Sometimes I just laugh. Mention the weather. Break the pattern. In that way you can proceed forward and not curve back around, repeating the pattern that is your usual way to respond to criticism and arguments.

Try it. It works. Suddenly you are in new territory.

**You are not your own type.**

I have to keep reminding people of this. They cannot imagine that someone they find interesting could be interested in them. They are missing all the clues.

Remember this: you are not your own type. That does not mean that someone much younger, much more amusing, much more whatever does not find you interesting.

I have a transvestite friend who says, "If you can't take rejection stay out of sales." Even if you're wrong a little rejection isn't going to hurt you. Believe me, there are people out there who think you've got it going on.

## "When you're pretty, it doesn't matter how you wear your hair."

This is something you say to yourself when you look in the mirror and are very dissatisfied with your appearance. I got it from the nightclub entertainer Frances Fay. She had a wonderful opening to one of her songs: "I'd like to dedicate this number to my ex-husband who is the drummer here in the band. We were married for a couple of years out in Chicago. I was a little heavier then but always a swinging chick."

She also said, "I have to get a younger band. It's so important towards the weekend." I was never sure quite sure what she meant—sexual hi-jinks or just plain fatigue? What I really learned from her is that instead of despair or self-dislike, you just have to laugh, don't you? Frances Fay. She was one of a kind.

## LIVING IN FRANCE

I first went to France in 1960. I went first to England and remember looking out the plane window as we were landing over that green country and thinking, "It really exists." Before then Europe was something I knew about only from books.

I actually flew from London to Paris and landed at Le Bourget, the same airport where Lindbergh had landed when he made that first crossing of the Atlantic. It was exactly as it had been in the 1920s. That was the only time I ever landed there as the new big airport to the south of Paris, Orly, opened very shortly thereafter.

It was dark by the time I had arrived at my hotel not far from the Champs-Elysees. I was determined to see Paris immediately. I took out my map and went to the Place de la Concorde, marched up to the Opera and came back down by the Tuileries gardens. I remember most clearly the strong smell of the gas from the taxis. London at the time still bore many marks of the wartime bombings. Paris, also, felt much as it must have immediately after the war.

Of all the European cities I have visited, Paris has managed to remain most itself. It has absorbed the tides of tourists while still remaining French, unlike places like Venice and Florence and Rome, which have almost become Disneyesque in their unchanging worlds.

A roundtrip flight to Europe was something like $300 in those days. Some of us got even cheaper flights on Icelandic Airlines, which required that you stop and shop at the airport in Reykjavik and then land in some small and remote country. But it was worth it. Wherever you landed there was going to be a direct train to Paris every day. And that was where I was going to go.

When I began a second career directing television commercials in Europe, I worked at first for an English company based in New York. I had studied French during the 1960s and could speak fairly creditably. So when the company called and asked, "Do you speak French?" I was able to answer, "As a matter of fact, I *do* ."

I reported for duty in Paris in 1970 and became a specialist in running water. Whenever a commercial required dishes in a sink or a whirling toilet bowl, I got the job. My background with Revlon and the beauty business didn't get me very far but the flowing aqua did.

I rented an apartment right on the Quai along the river across from Notre Dame. I had brought my cats with me from New York and there we were, ensconced on the third floor right in the heart of the city.

You are a different person when you speak in a second language. Standing in line in a crowded Parisian post office

I would say in French to the lady ahead of me, "Madame, this is no time to be buying commemorative stamps." And she would agree and depart. That was something I would never have done in English. Still would never do.

I learned, too, once I had a home in a small French village, that what the neighbors thought was of no interest. If you had an opinion different from everyone else in the village, you didn't care. They were wrong and you were right. Strangely, in this village, which was just on the southern edge of what had been occupied France, the only outcast was the plumber who had been in the French underground. They somehow felt he had let them down by not collaborating. That was how I interpreted it.

I had been renting houses in various parts of France in the summers while I spent three years there working as a director. I also traveled a lot doing commercials so I knew France pretty well after that time span. I had rented a little mill house one summer on the border of Pontlevoy, a little town in the Loire Valley two hours south of Paris.

After returning to New York to work again on the Revlon account at Grey Advertising, I continued to spend summers in France. The first year I returned I spoke with a real estate agent who said, "I have a house in a village in the Loire valley you'll never have heard of. Pontlevoy." I said, "Actually it's the only town I have heard of." I didn't like the rental house much but she had another to show me. It was for sale. Built in 1600. Directly across from the ancient abbey of Pontlevoy, facing the church of Our Lady of the Snows. I had not thought of buying a house but my niece, who was with me taking a break from modeling in Madrid, said, "Oh, Uncle David, you have to buy it!" And I did.

Thereafter I was entrenched in Pontlevoy. Charles De Gaulle was still running France. Telephones took two years to get. It was said that the General had never spoken on the phone. His wife did all the talking when someone called him privately at home. Phones were impossible to obtain because he disapproved of them. If you wanted to reach me you called the mayor of Pontlevoy. He would then send a small boy on a bicycle to get me. One had to hold the line as no one in the mayor's office could take a phone number as no one spoke English. Fortunately I didn't live very far.

As the years passed I bought a pair of small apartments in Paris in an old building that had been part stables, part living areas for the grooms who worked there. These real estate purchases were all very economical. Every summer I would go and renovate an apartment or one of the small houses I began to accumulate in the Loire. Coming out of a back road from the old city of Amboise I found a hillside of tumbling down houses. I eventually bought three and renovated them. I bought two more houses in Pontlevoy. One, the Maison de Dauphin, had been built in the 1600s when the heir to the French throne came for a visit. Another was the Vicariat, the only brick residence in Pontlevoy. This house was where the vicar lived, the assistant to the local priest, whose home was immediately adjacent. There was a connecting passageway on the second floor from the vicar's bedroom to the priest's. Hmmmmm.

My life for many years was deeply involved with rescuing old buildings and renovating them. I finally drew the conclusion that, "You can't save people but you can save houses." I suppose that means that when I die I will go to house heaven.

Now my life has also taken me to Uruguay in South America. I continue to save old houses. An old house at a low price is irresistible to me.

I have two takeaways from all my years in France:

1) The language you speak has much to do with your personality. You should really have more than one to understand who you are and who you can be.

And 2) though no French person wants to know you well enough so that you can call them in the night and ask for help, they still set an example of independence in their thinking. You can disagree with everyone and still be right. A great thing to know.

## You're not getting older. You're getting more sophisticated.

This is what I tell everyone I meet who is dealing with the years passing by. It is true.

At a certain point you have seen a lot. You have a very adult viewpoint. You are not going to be shocked by other people's behavior. As my manager says, "The party is over. Turn on the lights."

When you reach a certain age, you don't have to pretend anything anymore. Now is the time to live. To study what you haven't studied, to meet the people you have always wanted to meet, to sleep with the people you always wanted to sleep with. You are sophisticated now. Go for it.

## "When they get older, blondes must go south."

A maxim from my very wise friend Jean Ann Zuver. This is primarily for ladies but also applies to gentlemen. Jean Ann told me, "I have a friend who is confined to a wheelchair. She has long, beautiful blonde hair. She moved to Bogota where she is very popular. I guess in Bogota they realize that you can't have everything."

Try it. If you're not getting the attention you want in New York move to Miami. Then you can go to South America. I am blond and I went to Tierra del Fuego last year, the jumping off place for Antarctica. They were crazy about me.

## "There is magic in the streets of Montevideo."

Jorge Luis Borges

The river was brown, the streets empty, the atmosphere from the 1950s when I first saw Montevideo, the capitol of Uruguay, that little South American nation shaped like a piece of pie. Tucked in between the gigantic countries of Argentina and Brazil, no one you know will be sure quite where Uruguay is. But the magic was there, is there, for me.

You can't see it in photos, but there is a feeling that things will happen, things will work out differently in Montevideo. How they have worked out for you in other countries may not be the same here. It was true for me.

**When you miss your plane you never know whom you'll meet on the way back to the city.**

Who knows where life is leading? Instead of fuming and fussing about inconveniences and interruptions, perhaps the turns in the road are leading you in new directions.

This is not just Miss Goody Two Shoes talking, making the best of things. I think we are being pushed along a path and we're the ones who screw up by balking and dragging our feet because it isn't what we had planned and had in mind. Somebody or something great may be out there waiting and the encounter would never happen any other way.

**The good thing about hot weather is you don't have to use moisturizer.**

There is a good side to everything. If you live in hot weather as we have in Miami, you can console yourself about your inevitable dampness. It is great for your skin. I always think I look ten years older as soon as I go north.

## "Furs add ten years to a woman's age."

I don't like the idea that animals should be raised and killed so women can wear furs. I don't like ranting and raving either as in my experience confrontation rarely succeeds, particularly if there is money involved.

Your idea versus my idea? People find it hard to give in. So I prefer confronting one deadly sin with another. I just quote the famous society beauty Babe Paley who believed "Furs add ten years to a woman's age." She only wore beautifully tailored little cloth coats, often in bright colors. She always looked great.

Vanity will always win out over any other vice or sin. I do the same thing for smoking and drinking. "Who cares about your health, darling? But nothing puts more wrinkles in your face than cigarettes and booze."

People can shift in major ways when it comes to how they look.

**Always moisturize your neck. It may be your face someday.**

I don't mind going right out there and saying I strongly believe in plastic surgery. As the famous actress Ina Claire said to Noel Coward, "Get rid of that old stuff." When you look in the mirror and you don't like what you see, you don't have to put up with it. Pull that neck up. Get those dewlaps on each side of your mouth back up in place. Bags under your eyes? You don't have to have them. You don't want to be overly pulled up so you look like a window dummy. But age-appropriate surgery will put you back to what you looked like ten years ago. That's quite enough. Go for it.

# IN THE NAVY

I graduated from college at 21. Four months later, I completed Naval Officers' School in Newport, Rhode Island. That was it. From there I was sent to an aircraft carrier in the Pacific as a Communications Officer. There were thousands of us reserve officers with that same four months of training. Did the fleet really need all of us? Evidently. They kept piling them in for quite a few years.

My fraternity brothers who had graduated from the University of Michigan Engineering School with degrees in Naval Architecture and who had been aboard boats since they were four were all sent to landlocked jobs in various naval boatyards and never left the country. I with a degree in English literature did seventeen crossings of the Pacific in my first eighteen months of service.

My brother, who had graduated from the Naval Academy when I was sixteen, was in the submarine service and had never been outside the three-mile limit. After 18 months I was made a Junior Grade Lieutenant, up from Ensign. I was just one grade below him. He had been in the navy for ten years. It rankled him.

I always told people I joined the Navy because navy blue was one of my best colors. Which is true. And I looked good as an officer. I was a kind of Charlie McCarthy puppet for the crew's Edgar Bergen ventriloquist. I never tried to order them about. How could I? All the enlisted men in my Communications Division knew exactly what they were doing. As did the deck crew up in the little tower of the ship's bridge above the flight deck. The other junior officers used to say to me,"Why don't you have any problems like we do?" and I would reply, "I always do exactly what the sailors tell me to do."

I was aboard the USS Cape Esperance for more than half of my three years of duty when I was sent to Communications School in Monterey, California. There I was trained as a Cryptographic Officer, one who dealt with coding and decoding of messages. Reporting back to the aircraft carrier I was entitled to a transfer; I requested it and was sent to Bikini Atoll in the South Pacific for the hydrogen bomb tests, which were about to be conducted.

As has been recorded, the first test was six times larger than expected. A gigantic and fiery cauliflower shape just 35 miles away. The fleet was ordered to close all portholes and ports and steam to Eniwetok Atoll, some hundreds of miles away. We had many civilian employees aboard as the test was near the island where they were quartered. They never went back. The island no longer existed.

**You can only look ten years younger than you are.**

This is just some straightforward advice on extreme makeovers. I highly advise plastic surgery, but do not try for the impossible. If you really feel you missed out on your youth and you want to look twenty again, forget it. Ten years younger than you really are is possible. More truly isn't.

## Never turn around to look

You are the person other people are turning around to look at. Or not. It doesn't matter. If you must you can take a square look at someone else in public on your way to the bathroom. You didn't miss anything. Please, don't crane your neck as someone else passes by. Let them turn and drop whatever they're carrying when you cross their path of vision.

**"He was a man and I like that in a person."**

Mae West said this. The sentence could equally be "She was a woman and I like that in a person." Depending on where you want to go sexually.

Do you perhaps have too long a list of requirements before you allow yourself to become interested? Perhaps you should shorten it.

**A gay thought: the man lurking in front of the house, my nephew sees as a threat and a danger. I see him as a potential boyfriend.**

Need I say more? I think when you are a romantic you see life in much more positive terms. And gay men really are romantics. My great friend Quentin Crisp said in an interview, "Gay men basically want to have fun. Lesbians want to be right." It got him in a whole lot of trouble.

## I can be had… but I'm not going to tell you how.

Which means I may fall in love with you but I am not going to tell you how to go about it. You have to figure that out for yourself.

I have my weak spots, but you're going to have to get to know me. Well, I'll tell you one. I like a lover to be thoughtful. And I tend to fall for narcissists. The worst choice of all. No one is going to come between them and themselves. There, I told you something. The rest you have to figure out for yourself.

## Do not get involved with someone expecting them to change.

The only way they'll change is to get worse. If you love someone, love them exactly as they are. Do not expect your love to change them. It won't. You waiting and watching for them to change will only make them feel guilty. And as always, instead of accepting the guilt they will turn it around and for some reason you will be to blame. When you make people feel guilty they want to get you out of their life so they can stop feeling guilty. It's as simple as that.

## "You don't want to sleep with me. I'm terrible. Ask anybody."

This is a response to a sexual pest. I have a friend who also adds, "I hardly move."

You don't have a sexual pest on your trail? Perhaps you should get one.

## Crazy people can be great in bed.

I don't even want to tell you how I know this. But it is something you should add to your knowledge of the world.

**"You can look at my bankbook but I'll never let you touch my purse."**

I love these lyrics from the Bessie Smith song "Stingy Ginny." It's about people who see their sexuality as something to be traded for security and wealth.

Ginny sings, "Oh, I've got what it takes but it breaks my heart to give it away." It's the chant of those egocentric ones who will never care more for someone else than they do for themselves. Those who will never know the sexual fulfillment that love brings to a relationship. Narcissism is like this. No one will ever come between you and yourself.

**You pay with your purse or your person.**

Perhaps this is why we have so many working mothers, single mothers, working women in general these days. You should always be in a position where you can say "No" sexually.

**If you are not getting along with your lover, leave and come back as an attractive stranger.**

This is a quote from Margaret Anderson, a famous lesbian writer of the 1920s. She knew of what she spoke. Margaret was the co-editor of a famous literary journal and wound up in the South of France as the lover of a famous French actress. As you know, I think confrontation rarely solves any problem. Living with someone allows them to concentrate on things like the towels you left on the bathroom floor. Better to just hie yourself elsewhere and return as that embodiment of all they ever longed for.

**I have two rules:**
>   **1. When choosing a job take the one that pays the most.**
>   **2. When choosing a lover take the younger one.**

These rules are based on nothing but experience. The jobs turn out to be much the same. The salary is the consolation. The lovers tend to think more about you when they are younger and then there's the sex part. You have been advised.

## I'm sorry I can't come to your orgy. I'm claustrophobic.

If you live in New York you can add, "I can't even go on the subway." I just thought you might like to know how to get out of an invitation to an orgy gracefully. Then again, maybe you don't want to be excused.

## He doesn't want to give up everybody for somebody.

This applies more to men than to women. And not just gay men. We now have a whole generation of perennial bachelors, deep into their fifties, who are still playing the field. Men who love all the attention they get as potential suitors and lovers. They don't want to give up the attention they get from everybody to choose just one somebody.

Women are wiser. They know they have a window of opportunity despite the attention they may get heaped upon them. They will make their choice. Many men just cannot.

## "You can only feel happiness to the degree that you are willing to risk being unhappy."

This is from Erich Maria Remarque.I think it is true.

You want to fall in love with someone but you are afraid that you will be wrecked if you should lose them. You will. But you are never going to climb those peaks of emotion that love can bring unless you are willing to risk falling into the depths. Think about this, please.

I think a lot of people cannot connect with love possibilities because they are afraid of being unhappy. Don't be one of those people. Feel. Thrill. Suffer. It's called living.

# Part Three
Your Life In The World

**There are only three reasons to know someone:**
**1. They are beautiful.**
**2. They are interesting.**
**3. They are good.**

I always tell everyone. "If you are not beautiful and you cannot manage to be interesting I would highly advise you to be good."

The fact that someone can do something for you is not a reason to know them. That will always backfire on you.

## There are only 40 people in the world.
## The rest are walk-ons.

Researchers in Italy did tests in a business and discovered that 20% of the employees were doing all the work. The other 80% were pretty much along for the ride. They then examined a law office, a university, a hospital and a number of other activities and work areas. They found the results to be consistent. Twenty per cent were carrying the other 80%.

These are the forty people you know who seem to be doing all the moving and shaking. (Do you even know that many?) They are the people to whom you feel close and on whom you can count. However many you know, count yourself lucky.

## Never make a business call on Monday or Friday.

On Mondays everyone is struggling to catch up with the cascade of problems that have piled up over the weekend. On Friday they can't wait to get out of the office.

Tuesdays, Wednesdays and Thursdays are the days when people are far more willing to talk to you.

And another thing. Never call *anyone* before 10:30 in the morning. Glamour is impossible before eleven, Glamour is impossible before eleven. I repeat, glamour is impossible before eleven.

## IN MONTAGUE

I was brought up in a small country town. Although I am 84 years old I feel as though my life spans a much wider length of American history. The house I was brought up in was built in 1865. When I was a child in that house it did not have indoor plumbing or central heat. There was a privy in the garden and a pot under each bed for night time use. There was a large wood-burning range in the kitchen and a pot-bellied stove in the living room in the wintertime, which we carried out to the large red barn behind the house when spring came.

My mother had inherited this house when her parents died and we had withdrawn there in the Great Depression of the 1930s. We were not the only family to do this. There were many young families in Montague living in the large wooden houses that had been built during the logging boom of the late 19th century. Montague stood on a hilltop overlooking White Lake on its south side. The sister town of Whitehall stood on the opposite shore. White Lake fed into Lake Michigan some seven miles away, with its sweeping beaches and high sand dunes. Very much a kind of ocean, although of fresh water.

My mother was a Sumner, a descendant of one of the earliest pioneer families in this part of Western Michigan. Her great-grandfather, Putnam Wyatt Sumner, had come there to settle, having bought great tracts of land. He was named for a Revolutionary War general and had brought with him his mother, Betsy Hadley Sumner Brockway Clough, who was the daughter of a Revolutionary War soldier. In that way, since we discussed the family at great length all the time, I felt directly related to the first American war and had a relative whom I did not feel was so very distant, who certainly was alive at the time of the war or very shortly thereafter. Betsy had an ornamental metal marker on her grave as a true daughter of the Revolution. Every Fourth of July someone put a small American flag there. I remember this well.

My grandmother was a Gee. Her ancestor had been a British soldier who had come over at the time of the Revolution and had remained. Friends would sometimes come home for supper with me from school (we called it supper, as dinner was the noon meal on Sunday) and would ask later who all the relatives were whom we discussed at the meal and I would say, "Oh, they are all dead."

Montague during my years there still resembled the town that had been built rapidly during the logging boom. When Chicago burned much of the timber for its rebuilding came from our part of Michigan. When I was a child the large sheds that had stored timber still lined the road that led across the White River to Whitehall on its far side.

I graduated from high school with thirty-two students. Eighteen of us had been together since kindergarten and we all approved of each other highly. We saw more of each other than our siblings and I think we all left Montague High School, all thirteen grades in the same building, with solid self-esteem. We had all approved of one another for all those years together and saw no reason that the world would not continue to do so in the life that lay ahead of us.

## The trick is not caring.

I first saw this in a cartoon book. The artist had drawn a naked man strolling along in thin air above a crowd of naked men and women struggling along in varying degrees of unhappiness. The airborne man was smiling.

I took the cartoon's slogan "The Trick is Not Caring" and probably misinterpreted it as a method of dealing with the constant onslaught of criticism and displeasure I faced every day. I had it printed large and framed for my wall. And I pointed to it a lot when my staff was depressed by the absence of positive playback in their work.

You must care about the work but not care about the criticism.

I always gave positive playback but it was hardly enough in that wilderness of uncertainty where nothing was ever good enough. It worked fine and as I have written elsewhere in this book you do not have to care to do a high level of work. And if your work meets your standards of excellence, you can take your salary and go home with a smile on your lips.

**Always leave as though you are going somewhere more interesting.**

It's all part of creating a world around you that looks attractive to others. You are leaving to go somewhere you really want to go. Perhaps to be by yourself. Oscar Wilde said he liked reading his own diary because he always found dramatic stories fascinating. You are doing the same thing. You will find the world is quite interesting wherever you go, whomever you meet.

## "You know what I think? I think bullshit."

My friend Lucile Ormay said this one evening at the dinner table when the male guests were discussing sailing, their boats, races, etc. A number of us sat silent through much of the meal. Then Lucile spoke up, adding, "Are we going to spend the rest of the evening talking about boating?"

It suddenly put the evening on a whole other level.

## "And this is where you say, 'Oh, really?'"

A friend of mine was the chairwoman of some event for important New York women being held at the Waldorf Astoria some years ago. Special guests were seated at a table on the stage while everyone had dinner. Among these guests was the writer Dorothy Parker, who drank more and more during the dinner and by speech-making time was falling out of her chair.

My friend thought it best to escort her off the podium and to a taxi before she slumped to the floor entirely. She went to her and said, "Miss Parker, perhaps you'd like to go home now?" and dragging her upright pulled her offstage and started down the hall towards the elevators.

Suddenly midway down the hall Miss Parker pulled herself erect, recovered her composure quite completely and said, "As a matter of fact I must go home now and feed my little doggy." My friend was speechless and stared at her as she swept into the open elevator. Turning she looked at my friend and said, "And this is where you say, "Oh, really?"

This is a great example on how to deal with a surprising situation where someone is behaving outrageously or lying blatantly. You can even alter it to, "This is where I say, 'Oh, really?'"

It's an extremely useful expression.

## Never do walk-ons in someone else's movie.

I was invited to dinner in Paris some years ago by a wealthy friend. I was flattered. He was a self-made man. It promised to be an interesting evening.

Then he called back. He had invited some twelve other people to the same dinner. To show off his money? To have a rowdy evening?

I said, "Roy, I'm not coming to your dinner. I don't do walk-ons in the movie of somebody else's life."

## Generosity begets good fortune.

I always give to the first panhandler of the day. Just so I don't wind up there myself. And should I, at least I won't have to say to myself, "I deserve this because I never gave to beggars in the street." I would say, "What the hell? I always gave and here I am anyway."

This is one of the things that I have observed as life rolls along. When people need help, I help them. And I seem to have had very good luck. Some people have said I lead "a charmed life." I feel there is a connection there though there is nothing to really connect them. I always listen when my sub-conscious speaks.

## The greatest sin is being ungrateful.

I truly believe this. Those who have no real involvement with anyone other than themselves are guilty of this sin frequently. They are helped to find a job, lent money, taken to the doctor, endless varieties of being helped along through life. They never feel grateful and never say thanks. And they wonder why they are not helped again.

Sometimes someone you have helped very little will never forget and be very grateful. Which is great. Which is just to say, if you help someone don't expect to be thanked. You did it for the good of yourself.

## Men care most about what other men think of them.

In the 21st century men still care most about how they appear in the eyes of other men. Are they macho enough? Are they rich enough? Are they powerful enough? All men's goals have to do with how they are viewed by other men. Well, not completely. There are some academics and artists who rise above it.

Interestingly, women, who have in the past depended greatly on what men thought of them, are changing a lot. In the past decades they have banded and bonded together to start their advance to being men's equals. Which means they have started being concerned about what other women think of them. I guess this means that they are becoming more like men all the time.

**You can tell what a man is like by watching him walk away from you.**


Try it. Just watch a man walk away from you.

When he walks towards you he fakes it. Instead watch him walk away. He may very well walk like a big baby.

If from the back his head is up, his shoulders back, he strides forward, that's great.

## You can tell everything by looking at people's mouths.

People learn to lie with their eyes, but their mouths tell you everything. I've seen many men who had full mouths when they were young but whose lips disappeared until their mouth was nothing but a zipped purse. A man without lips is a man who will not give love.

If a person is older and still has lips, he is capable of giving. If his lips have been tucked away inside, he will not give. I have seen this many times. I know this.

**People complain to the same degree they feel they have no control over their lives.**

When you are running your life, you have little to complain about. When your life is running you, there is a lot to complain about.

People are drawn to those who seem to know what they are doing. Even if you don't, you can at least act as if you do.

## He has unwarranted self-confidence.

This is a personality style one sees everywhere these days. Young people and not so young who are very sure of themselves, a bit patronizing, very much at ease in the world. And one wonders on what basis? They have accomplished nothing, offer no evidence of being well educated, have no special plan for their future.

In a world that values little except appearance, money, and notoriety perhaps they qualify. The Kardashian model. There you have it.

## Everyone is more intelligent than you think they are.

This is my friend Jean Ann Zuver's belief. In this life, you will encounter people who think that others are not intelligent and easily duped and swayed. In fact quite the reverse is true.

Not everyone speaks well or is able to communicate what they think and believe. But in interfacing with others you would do well to deal with them as though they are smarter than they seem. You will be surprised at the results. And by their respect and liking for you.

## "Serious people act silly. Only silly people act serious."

Another pearl from Jean Ann. I think this is so astute. Life is so astoundingly difficult and dramatic the only thing you can do is laugh that you are still here having to deal with it. If you don't really understand where you are you will not find life laughable. You will think you can deal with it and make it work for you. Hello.

Beware anyone without a sense of humor and please don't marry them.

## The poor are like the rich. They live in the moment.

The rich don't worry about tomorrow because they have no reason to. Everything will be alright when they get there. The poor don't worry about tomorrow because everything is hopeless and it will be terrible when they get there.

Only the middle class, the *bourgeoisie*, worry about tomorrow because it might be good, it might be bad, and they will always be worried about what the neighbors think. The rich and the poor do not worry about what the neighbors think.

**I never want anyone to feel worse about themselves after I leave than they did before I arrived.**

I very recently read in another context, "No gentleman ever makes another person feel worse about themselves." That is the same thought and it is my number one rule in life.

I never want to damage anyone's self-esteem. I may not be here to make you feel much better about yourself but I am certain that I am not here to make you feel worse. Even if you would really like me to.

**The world is like a classroom of children with their heads down on their desks being obedient.**
**When you raise your head you discover there is no teacher.**

All those rules, all those people to please, all that conformity and similarity that society requires of you. You suddenly come to realize that it is yourself requiring this kind of behavior.

When you decide to go your own way and create a life that suits who you are, you find that no one notices or cares or if they do you don't even notice it

**"You don't have to be sleeping as long as you are lying down."**

This was my Mother's rule for her children if they were suffering from insomnia. Usually the moment you heard that it didn't matter if you were asleep or not, you promptly fell asleep. And furthermore, it is true. Don't worry if you are sleeping or not. As long as you are supine there in the dark you will be fine the next day. Really. She also used to add, "And don't lie face down and wrinkle your face!" She knew what she was talking about.

## I don't mind losing battles as long as I win the war.

Think about this. It applies in every situation. What do you want to accomplish? What is your end goal? You don't have to be right all the time or succeed at every step to get there. Letting obstructionists think they are winning can be a very good strategy. Being a smiling loser as you go along can be a very good way to work. Then suddenly: Bam! You're the winner.

## "He may be a lot of things but he's not bourgeois."

This is the nicest thing anyone ever said about me. I have tried hard to live my life without being concerned what the neighbors think. Someone (Susan Rothchild) noticed.

**"A child says nothing matters, but it takes an adult to say it doesn't matter that nothing matters."**

I love this quote from the novel *You and Me* by Padgett Powell. The only benefit I can see in growing older is that you have experienced pain and loss and unhappiness and you know you've come back from it. Knowing this helps you get through additional sieges of pain and loss and unhappiness. You also know that the fact that nothing matters has nothing to do with having a good time while you are here.

**"We are all in the gutter but some of us are looking at the stars."**

This is a quotation from Oscar Wilde that I had framed on my wall in my advertising office. We muck along, dealing with other people and all their infinite variations on the seven deadly sins, but that is not all there is.

There is beauty and there is hope and there is laughter and there is love and we can have all of these things in our lives. We just have to keep looking up!

**"The world is out to get you. If you're beautiful, even sooner."**

Andy Warhol didn't have a great opinion of the world. This was his quote. I just want to add, the world may be out to get you but it requires that you pay attention to them. They can't get you unless you care what they think about you. As you know, I strongly advise against this.

**"There is only one good life. It's the life you want and you make it yourself."**

Diana Vreeland, the legendary editor of *Vogue*, said this when interviewed for the recent documentary on her life. She was not a person I particularly admired but every once in a while she made a trenchant remark. Those remarks revealed that she had put together the life she wanted and that is something one has to admire about her, whether it was a life you would have wanted to have or not.

**I concern myself with what I think of other people, never with what they think of me.**

I am not for everyone. Neither are you.

Life is too brief to be rushing about trying to tailor oneself to the tastes of others who, for the most part, are not paying any attention in the first place. I mean this. Are you wasting your time catering to those who care nothing about you?

Remember, there are only 40 interesting people in the world. Do you know some of them? Good.

## RIGHT NOW

Because I am 84 I am frequently asked, "What was the favorite time of your life?" As though it is all over. I always say, "Right now."

I mean it. I like my life right now better than any other time although I liked the other times fine. I always tell people, "You cannot ruin your life after seventy." No one is going to say, "Oh, and he/she had so much promise." You are over seventy and you can do just as you please. Study guitar. Visit Guatemala. Go to a terrible bar. Being over eighty is even better. Then you can really do just what you want with your life. All your critics will be jealous.

I see 80 to 90 as late middle age. Maybe I'm wrong. It could be just middle age. I take no medications. There is nothing wrong with me physically. And I thoroughly enjoy writing and creating books that I don't think anyone else is going to do. I've done over twenty books, picture and otherwise. And they are all books other people would probably not do.

I also tell people when they bewail the fact that they are aging, "You are not getting older, you are getting more sophisticated." As the years pile up you are also getting a point of view younger people don't and can't have. You begin to perceive what really motivates people. You see that many of the principles of living here in the United States are quite different from other countries. Some of this is good. Some of it simply doesn't deliver a gratifying life to a lot of people. You can begin to develop your own philosophy and more important, act upon it.

My grandmother in her 40s seemed very grandmotherly. Now being in your 40s is post-collegiate. We are revising our ideas about what being seventy means. I have a friend whose mother just got a divorce as she approached that age. She has an entirely different idea of how she wants to spend the rest of her life.

The baby boomer bulge just hit sixty-five. I tell my more mature friends,"Come on. You could easily wind up living another thirty years. Are you going to just sit about? These could be the most fun years you've had yet."

I tell them to remember, "You are not your own type. You might not be interested in someone your age, but others are. Don't ignore the clues. Somebody could be coming on to you and you are just ignoring them because you don't think it's possible. And if you're wrong, who cares. No one ever died of embarrassment."

Relaunching my theater career has been great as well, as I write and appear in shows no one else would ever do. With success. We have a great murder mystery musical called "The Secrets of the Chorus" about a fading second-tier movie star out on tour in a show backed up by a chorus line of drag queens. We have songs about subjects most people are pretending aren't happening in their lives. I really enjoy doing the things that back in the 20th century were taboo or nearly so. We are now in the 21st century and it's a whole new ballgame. Electronic communications make hypocrisy harder and harder to get away with.

I read an interview with an author who said his children didn't like to find themselves appearing in his books. He told them, "If you don't want to read about it, don't do it." I love that about our own time. All those cameras trapping people doing what they said they didn't do. All those emails saying what they claimed they never said. Just assume that whatever you do, someone is going to know about it.

The great thing about adding up those decades is that you really don't care if they know or not. You are living your life so that when you finally lie down and let go you can say, "I did it. I really lived my life. Whatever experiences I wanted, I tried to have, whatever abilities I had, I at least tried to use them. I am ready to go."

23114237R00090

Printed in Great Britain
by Amazon